YOU'RE NOT ALONE

———

THE JOURNEY
FROM ABDUCTION
TO EMPOWERMENT

U.S. Department of Justice
Office of Justice Programs
810 Seventh Street, NW.
Washington, DC 20531

Michael B. Mukasey
Attorney General

Jeffrey L. Sedgwick
Acting Assistant Attorney General

J. Robert Flores
Administrator
Office of Juvenile Justice and Delinquency Prevention

Office of Justice Programs
Innovation • Partnerships • Safer Neighborhoods
www.ojp.usdoj.gov

Office of Juvenile Justice and
Delinquency Prevention
www.ojp.usdoj.gov/ojjdp

This document was prepared by Fox Valley
Technical College under cooperative agreement
number 2005–MC–CX–K116 from the Office of
Juvenile Justice and Delinquency Prevention
(OJJDP), Office of Justice Programs (OJP), U.S.
Department of Justice.

Points of view or opinions expressed in this
document are those of the authors and do not nec-
essarily represent the official positions or policies
of OJJDP or the U.S. Department of Justice.

The Office of Juvenile Justice and Delinquency
Prevention is a component of the Office of Justice
Programs, which also includes the Bureau of
Justice Assistance, the Bureau of Justice Statistics,
the National Institute of Justice, and the Office for
Victims of Crime.

This edition is the first printing.

INTRODUCTORY LETTER

I want you to know how happy we are that you have returned home. I also want you to know that you are not alone.

Every day, in communities across the country, children are abducted by people they know, by family members, by people they have met on the Internet, by acquaintances, and by complete strangers. It is estimated that more than one million children are reported missing each year. Fortunately, many of these children return home safely within a short period of time. Unfortunately, some do not return at all. And some children who return face major obstacles in their road to recovery and healing.

Several years ago, the Department of Justice, through its Office of Juvenile Justice and Delinquency Prevention (OJJDP), pledged itself to helping the victims of abduction, whether it be the families, the siblings left behind, or the children themselves. We have created resources to help these families cope with the aftermath of abduction and begin the healing process.

With the assistance of family members who have experienced firsthand the abduction of a child, OJJDP created a guide for families of missing and abducted children, titled *When Your Child Is Missing: A Family Survival Guide*—one of the resources most widely requested and used by families of missing and abducted children. In 2006, we created *What About Me? Coping With the Abduction of a Brother or Sister*, which helps siblings who were left behind cope in the aftermath of the abduction.

This third document, *You're Not Alone: The Journey from Abduction to Empowerment*, was prepared with the assistance of young adults who were themselves abducted as children and who are walking the path of healing and recovery. It is designed to help others who experience abduction begin to put their lives back together. Each abduction is different, and so is the path to recovery. And though the road to recovery is different for everyone, the destination is the same—to find empowerment and normalcy, and to live as full a life as possible.

It is my sincere hope that this document will help you on your road to recovery. I look forward to the day when we no longer have to search for missing children. But until that day comes, I believe that this document, and those that preceded it, will help children and families move forward on their personal journeys from abduction to empowerment.

J. Robert Flores
Administrator
Office of Juvenile Justice and Delinquency Prevention

LETTER FROM THE AUTHORS

Like you, we are survivors of abduction. We were abducted by strangers, by a parent, by someone known to the family, and by someone we believed was an online friend. Each of us had different experiences, which ultimately led us down different paths. Like you, we returned from those experiences and had to adjust to a whole new life.

Even though we are all survivors, we are also much more. We are college students, musicians, dancers, artists, athletes, and advocates. We are daughters and sons, brothers and sisters, boyfriends and girlfriends, friends, roommates, and community members. One day we will be husbands and wives, parents, teachers, forensic psychologists, and lawyers.

As you are all too aware, the journey can be tough. Our experiences—the abduction itself, our responses to it, and other life events—have shaped our lives in ways that we didn't always expect. We are who we are today because we chose to turn a negative experience into a positive one and to move forward on our journey from abduction to empowerment.

The paths we followed have not always been direct or smooth, but we have realized that the progression of life goes on. We want you to know that you can make choices and move forward, just as we have. We stood right where you are standing now—wondering what was in store for us in the future, how we were going to get there, and what we were going to face in the process. We are happy to tell you that we not only survived, but we have learned to thrive.

We have been where you are in your journey. You are not alone. As difficult as it may seem, you will get through this. It will get better. You will learn and you will grow. It is possible for you to continue on in your life and become who you want to be. We hope you will let us walk beside you as you go through your journey.

This book was created for and by survivors of abduction, with the guidance and assistance of the Department of Justice. We are telling our stories because we hope they will help you believe in yourself and give you hope for your future. Please know that what happened to you is your story, and you can tell it if you want, how you want, when you want, and to whom you want.

Always remember that the abduction was not your fault. You survived something that was out of your control. You can reassume control and, in the process, come out stronger. Your life is different now—there is a "new normal." That is what we mean by the journey from abduction to empowerment. It's the road you walk as you heal and grow, and learn to take back the reins of your own life.

We cannot say exactly how you should move forward. We can tell you, however, that your experience does not have to destroy your life. Our hope is that our words will give you encouragement and ideas about where to start. The most important thing to remember is that you have a life ahead of you and that it can be what you want it to be.

You are a survivor. We hope that you will choose to keep hoping, move forward, and recover your joy in life. Take care of yourself. Don't be too hard on yourself. The journey will take time. But you will make it.

Welcome home!

ABOUT THIS BOOK

In 2007, we were invited to be part of writing a book for others who survived an abduction and returned home. Many of us remember wishing we had someone to talk with in those early days who had been through a similar experience. We all knew that we wanted to be part of this project because we saw its potential to help others

> **"**One step at a time, one foot in front of the other. That's how you move on. There is something more for you to do ... you survived for a reason!**"** — Maggie

who were probably feeling as frightened and alone as we once did.

We came together with a team of professionals who had worked on similar documents to share our thoughts and ideas about what someone in these shoes would need to know. For many of us, this was the first time that we had a chance to talk to other survivors. We realized how important it was to connect with someone else who had a similar experience, even if all the details were not exactly the same. We hope that is what this book can do for you.

The book is divided into five sections, each dealing with different aspects of your personal journey from abduction to empowerment. The first section focuses on the journey itself and what you might expect along the way. The second discusses finding those who can help you through your journey. Section three is about retaking control of your life and making the choices that are right for you. The fourth section talks about roadblocks you may face in the process, and some possible ways that you can handle them successfully. The final section deals with finding the "new normal" in your life.

Each section includes a personal letter from one of us with our thoughts to help you through your journey. To make sure that we had input from as many different perspectives as possible, the team reached out to other young people who had been through similar experiences. Throughout the book you will see quotes from the five of us and from four other survivors of abduction—Josh, Lindsey, Sarah and Trevor. We want to thank them for having the courage to share their experience and taking the time to share their thoughts.

This book is a resource for you. Whether you read every word, skim pieces that grab your attention, or put it down until you're ready to look at it again later, we hope it helps you understand that you truly are not alone.

SECTION 1: YOUR JOURNEY

You may be picking this book up in the days following your abduction, or it may be months or even many years since your abduction. No matter where you are, how long it has been, or what level of healing you have found, it is okay. This is a journey—a process. Everyone handles it differently. Just know that as difficult as it may be, things get better. There is hope. What's important is that you are ready to hear from others who, like you, have survived an abduction.

You will have good days and bad days in the months and years to come. Sometimes you may feel your journey will never end. Sometimes it may seem you are retracing the same steps over and over. Some journeys take longer than others.

What is important is not to compare yourself to anyone else. The circumstances of your abduction and your survival were unique to you. Your healing process will be unique as well.

> " There's no sign that says you've arrived, you're here, but things do align and start working. It is possible to be happy. What you've gone through isn't the end of the world, because you're still here. We can't show you how to get over it, but we can show you it is possible. " — Sam

Your home life will probably be different and may never go back to the way it used to be. If you were gone for a while, or abducted at a young age, you may not remember what it was like before your abduction and you may need to get to know members of your family from scratch. Your routine, as you remember it, may be completely different now. You may feel that your abduction has become a point of reference—there will always be a "before" and an "after" this happened to you. This may be sad, frightening, and confusing all at the same time.

You may feel that you need some space to deal with what has happened, but that others do not want to let you be alone right now. You may feel torn between what you want and need, and what others think you want and need. You may want to talk, or you may want to be quiet. You may want others to be near you physically, or you may not want anyone to touch you. Sometimes all you want is to be alone, but at the same time you might be afraid of being alone.

You also may feel guilty for what happened, or others may make you feel that way. You may realize that your parents and siblings also experienced trauma, that life changed for them as well. As a result, they may have their own issues to work through. They may be overprotective or seem distant. It will probably take time to sort through everything and find the balance between what you need and what they need.

It will take time to process what happened to you. It took time for all of us as well. Although time really does make things better, it cannot make what happened go away. All you can do is choose to make the best of it, and to make an effort to turn the negative experience you went through into something positive.

We found specific strategies that helped us along our journeys. Keep in mind that the same strategies didn't work for each of us. As you embark on your journey, you will have to find out what works for you and what doesn't. Take your time, and trust your instincts.

For information on additional resources, please see "Where to Find More Help" on page 60.

" *Getting better doesn't always happen in a straight line. It comes and goes in waves, or cycles, like taking two steps forward and one step back. It's a journey you move through on your way to the other side. The important thing, though, is to keep going.* " — Tamara

TALKING TO SOMEONE

Talking about what happened is an important part of your healing. This is not something that you can handle on your own. You will find that many people will want to talk with you, and you may even feel bombarded by their interest in you. As you begin to open up, make sure that you talk about it in your own time and in your own way. Use this as an opportunity to take control of this portion of your life again.

Sometimes you may want to talk about what happened; other times it's the last thing you want to discuss. Remember that, apart from law enforcement's investigation of your case, you have to share only what you want to share, and only when you are ready.

When you *are* ready, find someone you trust. Some of us confided in our parents—their unconditional love and support has helped us throughout our journey. Others of us found it difficult to talk with parents and other family members who were also struggling with how to cope. Some of us who returned from a family abduction also found it difficult to talk with a parent or with other family members who were, in many ways, strangers to us. Many of us were successful in finding a counselor or therapist who helped us along our journeys.

We all learned that the key to finding someone to confide in was to find someone we trusted. This may have been someone who was helpful in our lives before the abduction, or someone new. We all found it important to find someone who was objective without being judgmental, who let us speak in our own voices and in our own time, and who had our interests at heart. It was important to find someone who could provide us with strength and guidance to help us make our own decisions.

Most important was finding someone just for us with whom we felt comfortable.

"Ignoring the problem doesn't help." — Alicia

Remember, you cannot do this alone. Asking for help is not a weakness. It is a strength and an important part of the healing process. Here are some of the people we turned to when we needed them the most:

>> Parents.
>> Brothers and sisters.
>> Other family members—grandparents, aunts, uncles, and cousins.
>> Best friends.
>> Boyfriends or girlfriends.
>> Counselors.
>> Clergy.
>> Teachers.
>> Coaches.
>> Friends.
>> Other trusted adults.
>> Others who had undergone similar experiences, like a support group.

Keep in mind that what you need may change from moment to moment, and that you may need to talk with different people about different aspects of your life and the abduction. Each of us found multiple people whom we trusted in different ways to help us with different parts of our journey.

> **" When something like this happens, it leaves a void inside of you. You basically have two choices: You can fill it with negative things, like alcohol, drugs, or promiscuity; or you can fill it with good works and a good heart."** — Alicia

FINDING POSITIVE OUTLETS

There will be times when you wish that things could go back to the way they were before the abduction, and times that you wish it had never happened. There will be times when your world seems grim. This is normal and to be expected. When you find yourself thinking, "What if?", engaging in activities that you enjoyed before the abduction may be a healthy outlet for your emotions now. You might also want to try a new activity to see if it helps. If it doesn't, try another until you find a positive outlet.

Here are some things that worked for us:

>> Keeping a journal.
>> Dancing.
>> Attending a class.
>> Painting and drawing.
>> Listening to music.
>> Reading.
>> Playing an instrument.
>> Exercising.
>> Playing sports.
>> Going to the movies.
>> Taking up a new hobby.
>> Going shopping.
>> Spending time with family.
>> Spending time with positive and good people because they will naturally bring you up and you will be likely to do positive things for yourself.
>> Setting a personal goal to do something new every day, even if it is something very small.
>> Spending time with friends who let you talk about it if you want to, but don't force you to talk about it if you don't.

> **"***Competitive running is what saved me. I had to get back to what I loved, back to what defined me. I fought so hard for it. I was not going to let my abductor take that away from me.***"** — Maggie

> **"***If you feel bad about yourself, do something that will make you feel good, like getting your hair cut, or something that you used to do before the abduction. Even if it feels weird. Spend time with other people, but don't be afraid to be alone. No one will heal like you, and patience with other people is the first step to your own healing.***"** — Lindsey

TAMARA'S STORY

Life, I have found, is not so much about the endpoint, but about the journey and how one responds to experiences along the way. It is filled with hidden corners, obstacles that may seem impossible to overcome, mighty triumphs, pain, fear, utter happiness, passion, and events one could never imagine until they become a reality.

I would like to share part of my life story with you, a story that begins when I was 16 years old and was kidnapped at gunpoint by a man I did not know. I open myself to you because we have two things in common. We were abducted and made it back alive, and we both have the ability to take back what was snatched from us—the freedom to live our lives.

The importance of telling you my story lies in the things I have done to empower myself in response to that experience. It lies in my journey, filled with hard work, healing, challenges, and triumphs over the trauma. As much as I would love to say that one day you will wake up and the work will be over, it will not. However, it does get easier with time.

I hope that sharing my successes and the mistakes that I have made in dealing with my abduction will help you on your journey. I have turned my own journey, although it has had its hardships, heartbreaks, and pain, into something amazing, not because I am a superhuman in disguise, but because of how I chose to respond to what happened.

My name is Tamara and I am 21 years old. I will be finishing my bachelor's degree in June 2008. I have been dancing since high school and I spend as much of my free time as possible out with friends, my family, at the beach, or curling up with a good book and my kitty. When I was 16, my life took an unexpected turn when I was kidnapped from my hometown.

Before that point I was an ordinary teenager—boy crazy like all of my friends, excited about my first real prom still a year away, and 2 years shy of graduating high school. I played sports, was a straight "A" student, and was always doing something goofy to make my friends laugh. The summer I turned 16 I felt on top of the world. A week after my 16th birthday, on July 31, 2002, when I was at a lookout point with one of my best friends, I was abducted at gunpoint and my friend was left behind, tied up. I was then to endure one of the most difficult experiences of my life.

A few hours later, my captor took another young woman. Together we chose to fight back and although we were unsuccessful, we did not give up. Approximately 16 hours later we were found, largely thanks to the success of California's first AMBER Alert. After he fired a shot from his gun, our captor was shot to death by the police. Moments later it was over. We were safe. We had survived.

THE FIRST FEW HOURS

We were first taken to the hospital to ensure that we were okay. Upon our arrival, we were taken inside on gurneys, covered head to toe with sheets. The media, via the AMBER Alert, had been airing our story from the beginning, and as a result everyone wanted to be the first to get a picture of us or catch us on film.

Everything became a rush after that. Detectives questioned us and put us into separate rooms as the hospital performed a full medical examination to collect any physical evidence. That experience felt like another violation all over again, but it was necessary. At the time I did not understand what was going on or why I had to undergo so many procedures. I was still in a state of shock from the reality of being kidnapped, and then the reality of being found.

" When I came home, everyone wanted to hug me. The problem was that I didn't want to be touched. At the same time, I understood that it was what they needed to help them heal and deal with what they had been through while I was missing. So, I thought okay, go ahead and hug me. And when I hugged my family, they also realized that I was uncomfortable and needed to be alone. We needed to reestablish boundaries. We needed time to figure out what was okay and what wasn't. "

Once they finished with us at the hospital, we were taken on a private plane back to my hometown. In the days following, I found that I had suddenly become a celebrity. My name and photograph were splashed across newspapers.

Because of the media attention, everywhere I went people recognized me. Some simply stared; others would whisper; some would approach me and say, "You're that girl." I became, in their eyes, that girl who was kidnapped in the summer of 2002. But I did not allow that to define who I was or who I am today. True, the experience is a part of me and has helped shape me, but in no way does it encompass all of me, nor will it encompass all of you. Although some people may try to force that identity upon you, we choose who we want to be—not them.

I chose to be grateful, not for the fame, but for the gift I was granted: the gift of seeing how much people cared, and how compassionate they could be. It's easy to forget that, especially after being kidnapped. But with this perspective I was able to see the vast amount of good there is in the world. So many people whom I never knew—and unfortunately may never get to meet—worked tirelessly to bring me home, as they did for you. That is something to think about. We matter that much to people—even ones we do not know, who were willing to do everything within their power to protect us. We were saved and are here for a reason. It's an incredible feeling to know that.

RETURNING HOME

Coming home, I faced many obstacles, some of which I still experience from time to time. I began to have nightmares every night, and could not sleep. It became extremely difficult to concentrate in school. Things that used to come easily for me suddenly became a monumental challenge. I was depressed. I cried countless times, but through it all I knew I had a choice. I could choose to dwell on how difficult things were or I could focus on the positive. First and foremost I was alive. I had another day to live, another day to make things that much better. Sometimes just getting out of bed was a huge challenge, but I did it every single day. That may seem like a little thing, but the little things make the biggest difference.

From the moment I came home, I chose to look at my abduction in a positive light. I chose to believe that good will always triumph over evil, that I came home for a reason, and that something phenomenal was going to come out of my

> " The day after I was rescued, I had to go with the detectives to try to retrace the steps, to take them to all the places where the evidence might be. That was extremely difficult. The last place I wanted to be was where it had all started. I had to relive it all, even though all I really wanted to do was to put it all behind me and move on. But I soon realized that putting it behind me was not going to be as easy as I hoped. I was able to take my brother with me to walk through everything, and that really helped. One of the most important things that I learned was that it is okay for you to say what you need. And it is okay to ask for someone to be with you if you want that. "

having been kidnapped and the hardships I faced. I believed that greatness could be found in the darkest of corners and chose to actively find that greatness.

As I was trying to cope with the negative emotions that were churning inside of me, especially the fear that things would not get any better, I made a conscious decision each day. I asked: How can I make today that much better than yesterday? I found that focusing on the positive eased the impact the negative parts had on me.

TAKING CARE OF YOURSELF

Through trial and error I also found that the best thing I could do for myself was to take care of each of my responsibilities. I was a student and therefore I needed to attend class, do my homework, and turn it in. I needed to eat three healthy meals a day. I had to sleep. I had to get out of bed, shower, and brush my teeth. I fought procrastinating and the tendency to want to curl up under my blankets and take a break from the world. Giving into that inclination and isolating myself from life and friends only made things worse.

During the bad times, I needed to reach out to someone whom I trusted and could talk to. That "someone" had different faces. Sometimes it was a family member, my best friend, a special person who had become a mentor, or my counselor. I found that talking to someone was extremely important for me. Speaking to a counselor or therapist helped me tremendously, but talking to

> *"Sometimes you just need to be selfish and do something for you. I know there are times when I just need to go out with my girlfriends, go to a football game or something and be carefree. I need that. If you're not taking in what you need, you don't have anything to give. You'll be stuck at a point of stagnation. Life's too short to be unhappy."*

friends and family enabled me to turn from the things that were bringing me down and focus on the positives. Most important, we would laugh together. Laughter and humor became one of the best outlets. Aside from a big bowl of vanilla ice cream, not much is better than laughter.

My counselor was very important to me—he helped me understand that these challenges were not permanent and to find positive outlets. He did not give me the answers, but he was there to help me find my own. This helped me trust myself—which is very important. The kidnapping had made me question my own judgment.

It was not as though I would never have learned to trust myself again, but my counselor helped me accomplish that sooner rather than later. He also helped me regain trust in adult males, for it was an adult male who had harmed me. More importantly, my counselor helped me understand that the man who took me intended to do harm to me, not all adult males. Realizing that not all adult males were my enemy helped ease my anxiety, for I sometimes thought that every adult male I met had ulterior motives.

The bottom line was, the man who abducted me took 16 hours away from me and I refused to let him have any more. I arrived at this belief only after my counselor and I worked through and made sense out of what had happened. Those of us who have had this experience have to navigate a delicate balance when it comes to looking back at what happened to us. We can choose to do so to help propel ourselves forward and take back what is rightly ours—the freedom to live—or we can use the memory as a crutch that pulls us down. I still use that thought as a sounding board to make sure I am on a positive road of healing instead of a road to self-destruction.

MAKING CHOICES

Even now as I tell you my story I am not finished with my recovery and healing, for it is a journey. It has revealed strengths I never knew I had. Yes, I felt like I was in pieces when I came home. But through constant hard work and choosing to remain positive in the midst of each challenge, I became whole again.

Some say that my work has helped me survive, but let me tell you, we survived when we made it home. Period. That process of survival is over. The journey from here on out is becoming whole, learning to live with passion, laughing with our whole heart and soul, and fighting for what we deserve, the absolute best in life. You and I are worth that and so much more. It is only a matter of whether or not we want it. It is a choice.

I have reiterated this notion of choice over and over because it is immensely important to me; it was—and is—my saving grace. As I struggled to deal with bad things in my family life as well as the abduction, I still had the choice to dwell on the negative or find the positive.

Making this choice every day in my life has not been easy. Every time I begin to think that it is too hard, I remember that I did not give up on myself when I was gone, and I will not give up on myself now. As my mother told me, "Yesterday is history. Tomorrow is a mystery. Today is a gift."

Each day brings us a gift: a blank slate. Our choices become the brush that paints each stroke of color. We paint our own picture and as we change our mindset, we change the picture, too. We choose who we want to be and how we want to be defined. I chose not to remain that 16-year-old girl who was kidnapped on July 31, 2002. Instead, I am Tamara, one who is making her own way in life. I am Tamara, one who has spoken out to the nation about her story and one who can be just as effective in her daily life with or without the speeches.

In my eyes, you are an incredible human being. I do not need to meet you to know this, for you have survived and that in itself is a true testament to your greatness. The amazing part about coming home is that we can be as ordinary or as extraordinary as we want. What kind of life do you want to live? The choice was mine, and the choice is yours.

Tamara

SECTION 2: CHOOSING COMPANIONS FOR YOUR JOURNEY

Learning to trust again is a huge challenge for anyone who has been abducted. Not only is it difficult to trust other people, it is often difficult to trust yourself. But we also know that you need people to walk this road with you.

Once you return home, your family and friends may not seem like the people you knew prior to the abduction. If you were abducted by a family member, chances are that you are returning to a family life that is totally different both from what you knew before the abduction and the way you were living until you were found. You may not know how to relate to a new family structure. If you have been gone a very long time, you may not know or trust the family you are coming home to at all.

When returning from your abduction, you, personally, may not feel the same as before. You may feel that no one truly understands what you have been through. You may not know how to explain it to them. You may be afraid of their reactions to things you might say, or you might want to protect them from knowing everything that happened to you.

Each of us was surrounded by different types of people after our abductions ended. The media spotlight was on us, at least for a little while. People heard about our stories in our towns, our States, and in some cases, across the country. These were people who we knew, as well as people who were complete strangers. Sometimes we were treated like celebrities.

> " Trust is really delicate, and if it is misused by somebody close to you it takes a long time to regain it. " — Sam

People stared at]us, felt free to ask prying questions, or just simply wanted to be around us. Suddenly everyone at school knew our names. Some of them wanted to be our friends, even though we never knew them before. We found out that some were genuine in their feelings, and some were not.

Remember:

>> Seek out the people you trusted before the abduction.

>> Communicate your thoughts, ideas, and needs to others.

>> Trust your instincts.

>> Establish boundaries about what you will and will not discuss.

>> Take it slowly.

>> Don't be too hard on yourself.

>> Don't feel pressured—trust comes in its own time.

" I was internationally abducted from Norway to the United States when I was 4 and returned when I was 18. I was a very different person from who I would have grown up as in Norway. I was a young adult and was not interested in giving up my independence. What happened was a slow and painful process getting reacquainted with my mother, my extended maternal family, and the culture I was estranged from. " — Sarah

REBUILDING TRUST

Rebuilding trust—in others and in yourself—is difficult. It can be tough to figure out whom to trust in these moments and to trust yourself to make good decisions. Regaining trust with yourself, family members, friends, or acquaintances will become an important aspect of every part of your life. How can you go about rebuilding trust?

" Trust is negotiated – you set the tone and expectations. "
— Tamara

First, start by seeking out and trusting the people whom you trusted before to make you feel safe. Those who were your true friends before will continue to be your true friends now. Communicate your ideas, thoughts, and needs to others, either by talking to them or in writing. We felt most comfortable gravitating to people who let us talk when we wanted or needed to.

> **"**I had to get to know my mother from scratch, while at the same time dealing with my own prejudices and fear I had built up toward this stranger from years on the run and the negative messages from my father.**"**
> — Sarah

If you were abducted by a family member and thrust into a whole new life, rebuilding trust can be extremely difficult. There are probably some very difficult feelings between your parents, and you may feel like you are in the middle of them. Returning to a different parent will force you to reevaluate your relationship with the parent who abducted you. You may need to establish a relationship with a parent or another family member you do not know. Take your time. Don't feel pressured into establishing a relationship within a few days; after all, relationships take time to grow. Even when it seems like it is taking a long time to get to know your new family, remember that you were found because they were looking for you. A bond exists, even though it may take a long time for it to feel solid. The key is to keep communication open, and to be honest with one another.

If your abductor was not a family member, it may still take a while for trust to rebuild within your family. Give yourself time. Speak with them about how you can reestablish a trusting relationship. Work together to make this happen.

When interacting with new people, trust your instincts about them. Take your time to get to know people. Don't force it. Don't be too hard on yourself if it doesn't come easily.

If others only want to talk about your abduction, they are probably not interested in you for the right reasons. Establish your boundaries about what you will and will not discuss, and whom you will talk to. Don't put complete faith in others the moment you meet them. Remember that building trust and confidence takes time.

> **"**You can't force trust, and you can't expect to feel it right away. You have to let it come to you.**"** — Sam

When dating, take it slowly and trust your instincts. Remember that how your abductor treated you is not normal. You should not expect—or accept—the same treatment from others. Many of us found, at least at first, that going out in groups was much better than individual dating. It allowed us to build confidence in ourselves, our decisionmaking, and our opinions about others, and to become more comfortable with the dating process. It also gave us the opportunity to let our friends help us feel safe in the dating environment.

It will sometimes be hard, but try to trust yourself. What happened was not your fault. Trust that your ability to make good decisions is still the same as it was before your abduction. In many ways, we believe we now make better judgments about others after going through this experience.

Trust your gut feelings about others, and about yourself. Whatever the action, if it does not feel like a good thing to do, don't do it. Keep the saying, "think before you act," in the back of your mind.

Sometimes it may take a while for trust to rebuild within your family as well. Give yourself time. Speak with them about how you can reestablish a trusting relationship. Work together to make this happen.

> "My advice to anyone who may have had a similar experience is to lay out a clear understanding with your friends, your family, and the people you let into your life. Tell them, 'Look, it makes me really anxious and stressed out when you ask me a bunch of personal questions. I don't want to talk about it and if I mention anything about my event or something that may trigger an old memory or something, don't respond to my rhetorical questions.'" — Lindsey

SAM'S STORY

My story is not your average, everyday story and neither is yours. My story is different from many of yours, but it is also similar in many ways. I lost 8 1/2 months of my life to a person that I am supposed to look up to and listen to. I lost 8 1/2 months of time with my friends and family to a person I am supposed to love and strive to emulate. I lost 8 1/2 months of my life to my dad. I was abducted by my own father.

On July 19, 1997, my dad took me from my mother. I was 10 years old. My parents had been divorced for some time when suddenly, my dad decided to take me away from everything I knew in my life. We traveled from one side of the country to the other, and when we finally settled in one place, reality sank in for me.

> **"Coming home from your abduction is half the battle. We were strong enough to make it through the hard part, but the road ahead is yet another struggle. You might think that when you arrive home from being kidnapped, everything is going to be okay and go right back to normal. But life isn't the same."**

I was not allowed to talk to others. I could not go to school. I couldn't even use my real name. We had to change our names and live a lie to make sure nobody would find us. But on March 28, 1998, in Alvin, Texas, I was found.

You were found, too. That is what makes our stories so similar. We were found for a reason. We were given the gift of coming back to our lives, and now it is up to us to make the most of it.

FAMILY ABDUCTION

When you are abducted by a family member, as soon as you come home you realize the differences in the way your family is structured. Your experience has affected your life and the lives of others. If you were abducted by a family member and returned to your other parent, your home, your friends and school, and your everyday routine all may be different. The list goes on and on. What you were used to for days, weeks, and even months before is suddenly changed. But, I am here to tell you that it can be okay.

Was it hard for me? Of course it was. It took me a long time to realize that my dad was not going to be in my life again. It is hard to lose somebody, especially when you know this person **could** still be in your life. But I had to ask myself if I really wanted someone in my life who was not going to do what was best for me.

> **"** *I think that the bottom line is that no matter who takes you, whether a family member, acquaintance, or stranger, that person is not a friend to you because they are not looking out for your best interests.* **"**

LEARNING TO TRUST

One of the biggest issues I faced was learning to trust people again. It felt almost impossible for me to trust anybody, even myself, after my dad deliberately took me away from my life. I didn't know who was really looking out for my best interests anymore. I found it very hard to realize that other people were different from my father, and deserved my trust.

You may feel the same way. I didn't trust people—really anyone—for a very long time. Then, I realized that there are people around me who really do love and care for me. There are genuinely good people out there who deserve my trust. Amazingly, rebuilding trust does happen. It just takes time. Don't be afraid to give yourself time, or to ask for it from those around you. Help them understand what you need.

Being abducted by a family member means that you are also suffering the loss of someone who was a part of your life but will not be in your life anymore.

I eventually realized that was okay. I looked for other people to fill the role my dad once occupied in my life, like my older brother, my basketball coach, or my friends' fathers. When I started trusting people again, I found they were there for me to depend on.

There are certain things that we all look for in people to see whether we can trust them or not. Honesty. Compassion. Concern. Love. You cannot force yourself to trust people. It takes time. How long? I cannot say. Each of us is different. When you have been in a situation such as mine you find that you pay closer attention to what people say and do and how they act, and you become very sensitive to people who betray your trust or even tell little white lies. All I can say is that it is possible to build trust in others again, and in yourself.

Remember that what happened to you was not your fault. Also remember that you were found because someone really loved you and had your best interests at heart. That is a huge thing. Try not to let what happened to you change your ability to see goodness in others. Surround yourself with people who make you feel comfortable and safe. Trust will come to you. Don't force yourself—take your time.

At first, you may feel lonely and that nobody is there for you. I felt that way for a very long time. Sometimes it can feel like no matter how much you talk about it, nobody will truly understand what you went through. This is when you really need to find someone who you are comfortable with to help you through this—a parent, a trusted adult, a counselor, a mentor.

> *Eventually you will realize there are people there for you; otherwise, you would not be back home where you belong.*

FACING THE PARENT WHO ABDUCTED ME

I also had to think about facing my dad again. For a long time I did not want to see him. I was angry at him for what he had done. But I heard someone else whose father had abducted him talking about how his father died before he had the chance to face him—and how he regretted never being able to talk about what had happened. I didn't want that to happen to me.

I realized that ultimately, I needed to see my dad on my own terms and in my own time. My dad had reached out to me when I turned 18, but I didn't see him until I was 20. Even after I decided I wanted to talk to my dad, it took me a long time to do it. I had so many questions: What would I say? How would I react? What would he say to me?

If you are not ready to see your parent, don't force yourself. Don't rush into it if you can't handle it. Figure out what is best for you, and then trust your instinct and follow your heart. As nervous as I was, once I did it, I was so glad I did. Afterwards, it was like I was released to live the rest of my life.

Don't let your abductor dictate the way you live your life, especially your relationships with other people. As I said before, learning to trust again will take time—it is a process—but in time it will be a positive thing because you have the rest of your life to live.

SECTION 3: GETTING IN THE DRIVER'S SEAT

You've experienced something traumatic that was out of your control. As difficult as it may be to realize, you have an opportunity to turn that situation around, to take back control of your life. Things are different now, to be sure. But that doesn't mean you can't still live the life you want to live.

Though at times you may not realize it, you do have choices, and you can make good choices. You can take the negative things that happened to you and turn them into something positive.

The word "empower" means to give power or authority to, to enable, to permit. Empowerment does not happen overnight.

At first when you return following the abduction, your life may be turned upside down. Your emotions may be out of whack—you may be upset, angry, ashamed, confused—you may be all of these things and more. You may worry about the effect this will have on you now and for the rest of your life. You may worry about what others may think about you, how they will respond, and if you can ever move towards brighter days.

This is what happened to us. But, eventually, we all came to a moment in our journeys when we decided that we would no longer let what happened to us dictate who we were going to become.

> **"** *You've been a victim of some-one else's choices. But there's a difference between being victimized and remaining a victim. A victim is one who remains at a place of stagnation, who never moves forward from what happened; a survivor is one who takes the necessary steps to move forward, to heal, and who is not defined by what happened.* **"** — Tamara

This experience happened to us, it is a part of our past, and it will always be part of who we are. But it doesn't have to be our future. This was the moment we really began to gain control of our lives again.

WAYS TO REGAIN CONTROL

Each day you will have an opportunity to decide whether to be in control or to let what happened control you. It's not an easy decision, particularly when you first come home. There are ways you can do this:

>> You can choose to get up each day, put one foot in front of the other, and do the basic things you need to do.

>> You can reestablish boundaries in your life in a way that makes you feel comfortable.

>> You can take back some of the things that were stolen from you— your dignity, your confidence, your sense of humor.

>> You can choose to can go back to your old school, to transfer to a new school, or to be schooled at home.

>> You can tell others what you need, not what they think you need.

>> You can—and should—ask for help.

>> You can choose whom you want to be with at any time.

>> You can choose whom you trust and whom you do not.

>> Your ideas for regaining control:

YOUR RIGHTS

Remember that you have rights and that exercising those rights can help you stay on course and maintain control over your own destiny. Here are some things that we wish someone had told us in the early days after we came home:

1. YOU HAVE THE RIGHT TO YOUR OWN STORY.

What happened was not your fault. It was out of your control. But you have an opportunity to regain control. Your story is yours alone. You can control how it is told, and to whom.

2. YOU HAVE THE RIGHT TO YOUR OWN FEELINGS.

If you are mad, scared, numb, nervous, happy, feel like crying, or have any one of a thousand other emotions, that is okay. You might feel opposite feelings at once—happy and sad, relieved and scared, angry and peaceful. Your feelings are your own, and it is okay to feel that way.

3. YOU HAVE THE RIGHT TO FEEL SAFE.

If something makes you uncomfortable, don't do it. Trust your instincts. If you need help from others to make you feel safe, ask for it. Don't be afraid to say no. Tell someone if you do not feel safe.

4. YOU HAVE THE RIGHT TO TELL OTHERS WHAT YOU NEED.

Speak up for what you want. Tell others if you need to talk, want to be alone, need a hug, don't want to be hugged, etc.

5. YOU HAVE THE RIGHT TO KNOW WHAT IS HAPPENING TO YOU AND AROUND YOU.

Ask questions until you are satisfied with the answers. Doctors, nurses, police officers, social workers, prosecutors, parole boards, and others should tell you what is happening, as many times as you need to hear it, until you understand what is going on.

6. YOU HAVE THE RIGHT TO HAVE SOMEONE YOU TRUST HELP YOU THROUGH YOUR JOURNEY.

You can ask for a parent, a trusted adult, a counselor, an advocate—someone who has your best interests in mind—to walk with you through your journey. Seek out the person(s) whom you trust who can help and support you, and don't be afraid to tell others if they are not filling that role.

7. YOU HAVE THE RIGHT TO YOUR OWN PERSONAL SPACE.

You have the right to establish your own boundaries and make them clear.

8. YOU HAVE THE RIGHT TO SAY NO.

You can say, "I don't want to do that," or "I don't want to talk about that," if and when you need to. This applies to everyone in your life. You may not be ready to talk at any given point. Keep in mind, however, that sometimes questions, uncomfortable as they seem, are being asked by people who are doing their job. If you don't know why you are being asked a specific question, ask why it is important.

9. YOU HAVE THE RIGHT TO DECIDE IF AND WHEN YOU WILL TALK TO THE MEDIA.

Talk to the media when you want to, on your own terms. You have no obligation to speak with them. You can decide what you will and won't talk about. Talk to an adult you trust about how to handle the media.

10. YOU HAVE THE RIGHT TO MAKE CHOICES IN YOUR LIFE.

The journey from abduction to empowerment is about choices—choices in terms of what you do, when you do it, whom you do it with. Sometimes choices are very difficult. That is when you need to ask for help in making decisions. But you always have the right to voice your opinion about choices. That is empowerment.

> **"**One thing that really helped me was when I was forced to make a decision, whether it was easy or hard. I had to get out of 'robot mode' and think for myself. I had to decide what I wanted ... like even picking out the color for my room. My parents hated the color but I loved it because it was something I wanted, and something I decided.**"** — Lindsey

ELIZABETH'S STORY

Believe it or not, you are a champion. We all face trials and challenges in life. Some are more difficult than others. You and I faced a very difficult one and you, like me, have triumphed over this trial. You have a new, and different, life now—a new normal. This new life can be something good if you make it that way.

My name is Elizabeth. Currently I am 20 years old and a music performance major in college. I love to ride horseback and spend time with my family. Like you, I am also a survivor. The night before I was to graduate from junior high I was kidnapped from my bed at knifepoint. I was held captive for 9 months until I was rescued. My life has never been the same since.

Many aspects of my life have changed, as I'm sure yours has. Much about an experience like ours can overwhelm us when we come home: the media, the notoriety, the mixed emotions, our families, school—the list could go on forever.

> **"This is important to remember. You were found because someone was looking for you! You were not then, and you are not now, alone. You are here because there are people who care for you."**

But even through these experiences and the changes that result, it is important to remember that just because something bad happened to you, it doesn't mean you are bad. You are still entitled to every possible happiness in life.

When I came home, I had no idea just how big the search for me had been. To this day, 5 years later, people still come up to me and tell me how much they searched for me and prayed for my safe return.

MAKING A CONSCIOUS DECISION

I made a conscious decision that my abductors had already taken away 9 months of my life, and I certainly was not going to give them any more time than that. We all have so much to live for. It is not worth living in the past. Each of us has so much potential in this world. I find it hard to believe that one experience can hold us back from being the individuals we want to be and stop us from doing the things we want to do. I know this can be a struggle for many kids who experience what we did. Hang on. Keep moving forward. Take one step at a time. It will get easier.

One thing that I realized was that I could be in control of my own thoughts and feelings. Many people will want to pry and ask questions. Do not feel obligated to tell people your experience unless you want to. Most people do not want to hurt you; they are just curious and do not realize how to act or to treat you. But just because they ask, or do something nice for you, does not give them the right to know what you went through. What happened is your story, which you can choose to share or to keep private. You have the ability to choose what you want to say or do.

> *Find someone who you know genuinely cares and wants what's best for you. This person may be a family member, a friend, a mentor, or a counselor. Find that person who has your best interests in mind, and with whom you feel you can totally be yourself.*

We all have different ways of getting through our experiences after we come home. One of the ways I did this was to set goals, to work continually toward those goals, and then to set new ones. Finding healthy emotional outlets helped me a lot as well. One of my outlets was playing my harp. I could put my soul into my playing, which in return, for me, expressed how I felt better than talking to someone might have done.

REACHING OUT

When I needed someone, my family was incredible. Both my parents did more for me than anyone else could—they would have gone beyond any boundary for me. Another important person who really helped me was my grandfather. We would go horseback riding together and talk about geography, history, religion, politics, genealogy, animals, his life experiences … anything I wanted. He was able to give me guidance because he genuinely cared about me.

Another important part of coming to terms with my abduction was my faith. Having faith has helped me to understand some of the reasons why I had to go through what I did. In my experience, having religion as a part of my life not only helped me understand my trials better and brought me comfort, but it also provided a support group for me from other members of my faith.

Elizabeth

> "In the end it all it comes down to our choices. Time is always passing and we have the option to stay in the same place forever or move on. As we move forward in our journey, life can continue to be everything that we want, even if it is different than what we thought it would be. I wish you a successful journey filled with many good choices. Lead the kind of life that you can look back at one day and say, 'Wow, what a life!'"

> "I remember going hiking with my parents and some other close family members, up into the part of the woods where I was kept all those months. My mom asked me if I was ok, and I said, 'I feel triumphant!' This is where I was held hostage, and now I'm showing you. They can't have this anymore."

SECTION 4: NAVIGATING THE ROADBLOCKS

As time goes on, you will learn to navigate this new course and things will get better. That doesn't mean that it's going to be easy, or that there won't be difficulties. You may be faced with some bumps along the way that can be seen as nuisances or even major obstacles. There will probably be more than one opportunity to let yourself get sidetracked on this journey.

Just as you feel that you are getting to your new normal, there may be events that seem to set you back—occurrences that trigger thoughts and emotions and turn your memory back to the abduction.

Sometimes you may not know what triggers your memory, and sometimes you may. For us, these triggers were as simple as the smell of grass, a Coca-Cola can, a tollbooth on the turnpike, a red-haired man, a father with a 10-year-old son. They were also as complex as facing the abductor, revisiting the crime scene, or seeing the picture of another abducted child.

> **"If you feel out of your comfort zone, don't be afraid to get away from whatever is making you feel awkward, but don't worry about it either."**
> — Lindsey

You will not always know when you are about to come face-to-face with one of these triggers. But when they happen, look toward those you trust to help you through them. Take your time and find a safe place to cope with these emotions.

Other circumstances made us get off track as well, ones that we did not realize we might face. Here are some of the events that you may also have to deal with and how we learned to navigate around the roadblocks.

POST-TRAUMATIC STRESS DISORDER

Many young people who were abducted have to deal with Post-Traumatic Stress Disorder (PTSD) afterwards. This is a normal response to the kind of trauma you have experienced. PTSD can show up in different ways—you may feel fine one moment, then anxious, nervous, or uptight the next. You might experience nightmares or flashbacks. You may not remember everything that happened, and you may block out things that happened even before you were abducted.

> " You can't control when you see or experience something that will remind you of what happened. You can't stop the world and say, 'OK, from now on I can't see any of this or be around any of that...' But you can do your best to avoid triggers. You learn to recognize them, anticipate them, and cope with them." — Maggie

These moments of anxiety or panic can hit you out of the blue. Something ordinary—everyday sights, smells, sounds, or words can trigger one. You often won't know what is a trigger for you until it has happened.

Not everyone will have PTSD, and no two people will have it in exactly the same way. The important thing to know is that it is a natural response to the kind of experience that you have been through. Talk to someone you trust—a trained professional, a parent, a counselor, a teacher—about what you are feeling and work with them to find help. There are ways to help you deal with it and learn to cope. Don't put added pressure on yourself to feel like you must deal with this by yourself. Most people can't do it alone, and there are people who can help you.

> " I know I suffered from some symptoms of post-traumatic stress disorder but I don't think that I even knew what it was. I remember that I couldn't sleep in my own room alone. I always either slept on my parents' floor or I had to have a friend to sleep by me." — Trevor

> **"** I only go on media if I believe there's a good purpose for it. I didn't go on any media when I first came home, and when I finally decided to, I didn't go on alone. If you don't feel like you're ready for it, you don't have to. You can just say no. It's not like it's a once-in-a-lifetime opportunity. The media will still be there if you decide later you want to talk about your abduction. If you do decide to talk, let the media know where you stand, and don't let them walk all over you. You still have rights as a human being. You have the right to tell them what you are or are not willing to talk about. **"** — Elizabeth

DEALING WITH THE MEDIA

In many instances the media play a big role in bringing children home. They can get the word out about an abduction, who might be responsible, what kind of car was used, and where the abductor may be heading. They can help the police notify the public about your abduction and can help issue an AMBER Alert. The problem is that sometimes the media attention does not go away once you are recovered. The media will want people to see that you are okay, and to find out exactly what happened to you while you were gone. People may feel like they have invested something personally in your life. And they may have—they probably thought about you, worried about you, prayed for you, or maybe even joined the search for you.

As true as that might be, you do not have a responsibility to them. Your responsibility is to help yourself heal and to do what is best for you.

> **"** I started writing down answers to questions after talking with my dad. I wrote down things I should say if I didn't quite know what I was feeling. I didn't want to hurt people's feelings, but felt that I did in the process. This helped me deal with their questions and feel better about me as well. **"** — Lindsey

You can choose whether or not you want to tell your story or how much of your story you want to tell. You can choose when, where, how, and to whom it is told.

> *" The truth can easily get misconstrued, especially in the media. Always remember that it is your story, it is your life, and you can pick and choose what you want to do with anything. It's ok to say no. "*
> — Tamara

Do not feel obligated to talk to the media. Have your parents or people you trust help you make decisions about interacting with them. If you feel there is a good reason to talk, then tell the media what you want to say. If you don't, then say no.

You can also write down automatic responses to questions that you receive repeatedly, or those you think people will ask you. This will help you sort through your thoughts, express your feelings and emotions, and become more comfortable when questions come out of the blue.

If your story did not receive media attention, it does not mean that what happened to you is any less traumatic than what happened to anyone else. You can be grateful for the opportunity to heal in private. Take advantage of the quiet space in which to make your choices about your future.

>> Your automatic responses to questions:

POLICE INVESTIGATIONS

One thing that can be very difficult is telling the police everything that happened, whether it is right after you were recovered, or days, weeks, and months down the road. Sometimes an investigation can continue for a long time. There are moments when you feel like you've just returned to some kind of normal when the police show up to ask more questions and you have to relive the events again. This can be frustrating and confusing, and may even make you angry.

> **"** *Telling my story to the police was one of the hardest things I had to do right away. But the police officers who interviewed me were great. They were in street clothes, which helped. They addressed me by my first name, which was huge. They listened and focused their attention on me. They were very thorough, but they let it come out in my terms.* **"** — Maggie

Whenever you talk to the police, try to keep in mind that asking questions is part of their job. Answering their questions is an opportunity to take back control of your life. Whatever you can tell them will be helpful in stopping what happened to you from happening to anyone else.

Be prepared: They are going to ask you graphic questions. Try to remember that they are there not to attack, but to listen. As hard as it is, it's important to answer all of their questions honestly. When it seems like they are asking you the same thing over and over, as though they did not hear you or believe what you are saying, remember that they are trying to find out everything that happened.

When you meet with law enforcement, take your time. Ask for what you need to feel safe as you answer their questions, whether that is having someone in the room with you or asking someone in particular to leave the room. Trust what you remember about the event. You are the only one in the room who was there. Give yourself time and tell them everything you can. Ask them questions if you do not understand what is going on or why they are asking specific questions.

FACING THE PERPETRATOR

Some survivors may have to face their abductors again. Every situation will be different and every survivor will handle the circumstances differently. If you were abducted by a family member, it will feel very different to face your abductor again than if you were abducted by a stranger.

Survivors often go through the legal process to see that justice is done and face their abductors in that way. This can be incredibly challenging. Try to keep one thing in mind as you go through this: You've won. No matter what the outcome, you've already won. You are here, you survived, and you are moving on.

THE COURT PROCESS

Not every survivor of a crime has a chance to see justice done in court. If your perpetrator is caught, you are lucky. But that may mean that you have to face them in court. Although this may seem to be a negative, it can actually be a tremendous opportunity—one that you should consider taking full advantage of.

Going through the legal process can represent a milestone in your recovery. But it can also be fraught with many emotions. Don't feel bad about not wanting to go through a trial or face your attacker. The reality is nobody wants to go through a trial.

> **"**I wish I had someone there for me and just for me...I wish I had a social worker just for me, who would do things just for me because I needed or wanted him/her to do it. Things like talking to the judge, or just getting things done. I was sick of stalling.**"** — Josh

The best thing to do in this circumstance is to ask someone to help you through the process—an advocate who is there solely for you, to explain what is happening and to 'hold your hand' through the legal proceedings of your case. Ask the police for the names of victim advocate programs in your community to help you through the legal process.

VICTIM IMPACT STATEMENT

At the sentencing phase of your trial, as the survivor, you will have the opportunity to give a victim impact statement. This is your opportunity to say how you feel and how this experience has changed your life. Impact statements are given just prior to sentencing and are intended to influence the sentence the judge imposes.

Preparing your statement. Hopefully you will be notified of your right to give an impact statement well in advance of the day of sentencing so you can prepare what you want to say. You don't have to recite your statement from memory. You can write it out or type it. This is an experience that may trigger all sorts of emotions and bring back many memories. You may have a hard time standing up in a courtroom full of strangers and reading it to your perpetrator.

Here are our words of advice:

>> Give yourself plenty of time to prepare it.

>> Go slow when you make your statement.

>> Try not to be afraid of the perpetrator. You will be well protected as you read your statement. There will be plenty of physical distance between you.

If you want to make a statement but do not wish to speak, that's fine. You can have an advocate or designated family member be your representative to speak on your behalf. You don't even have to prepare a statement at all if you choose not to.

What do I say? You, as the survivor, are free to say pretty much whatever you want. This is your chance, through your demeanor and voice, to reveal to the world what kind of person lives beneath the surface. But a word of caution. Preparing your statement is completely different from actually delivering it with the perpetrator standing there. Your emotions may be high and very raw; that is to be expected. Cry if you need to. Take your time. Hold your head high if you can. You've worked hard on your journey to get to where you are at this point. Remember that the fact you are standing there with the ability to give the statement means that you have already won, regardless of the outcome of the trial.

PAROLE HEARING

Years may pass and then all of a sudden your perpetrator may be up for parole. Suddenly emotions may surface and you may once again face your feelings from years ago. At this time, the media may come back into your life, even though you felt you had reached a "new normal."

> " My abductor tried to destroy my life and it's now my mission to prove that he failed to destroy me. I will not let him win the battle of taking my spirit, even if he tried to take everything else." — Lindsey

You have the right to be notified when your perpetrator is up for parole or is being released. You may have an opportunity to speak to the Parole Board before the hearing if you want.

You can send letters to the Parole Board expressing your thoughts about the potential release of the perpetrator. Others can send letters as well. Know that your words and letters to the Parole Board can make a difference. It is once again your opportunity to take control and to let others know your feelings.

MAGGIE'S STORY

My name is Maggie and I am 29 years old. I was born and raised in Ohio, where I currently live. I obtained a communications degree from Defiance College in 2001. I was the inaugural recipient of the NCAA Inspiration Award in 2002 in Indianapolis. Currently, I work full time as a victim advocate (specializing in domestic violence) with the city prosecutor where I live. In July 2008 I will graduate from Capital University Law School's paralegal program with a paralegal certificate, and I hope to further my career in law.

It has been a long and difficult journey to this point, as I know it has been for you. I want to congratulate you; you're courageous and already have come a long way. Your abduction is over. The worst is behind you. I hope, as you read this document, that you find strength and determination as well as some answers.

> *" Through different circumstances, I've traveled a journey similar to yours. Just like you, I'm trying to find the 'new normal' in my life. Just like you, I am a survivor. And just like me, you are not alone in your journey."*

I want to tell you a little bit about my story, and about things that can pop up along the way and threaten to detour you as you move along in yours.

Throughout our lives we constantly ask ourselves, "Who am I? Where do I fit in? What do I have to offer the world around me?" I was asking these questions at the end of my freshman year in high school. Desperate to put a difficult year behind me, I tried out for the local cross-country team. It was there that I found my niche. I loved being a student-athlete. I embraced competitive running. I took immense pride in that role and the responsibilities that came with it. I loved who I became as a runner. And I loved cross-country.

On Friday, September 16, 1994, a date I will never forget, the team and I started our run at 6 a.m. As we had routinely done for the past 3 weeks. I felt safe running the streets of my hometown. So safe that, at the 3-mile mark, I turned back early and headed back toward the school. With my headphones blaring I ran the well-lit streets, retracing my route back to the high school. I wasn't more than a mile away from my destination when I was grabbed from behind by a man and pulled into an alley. He forced me at gunpoint back into a wooded area behind the local YMCA.

About that same time, my mom was taking a walk with a friend. She suddenly stopped, having a strange feeling that something was wrong. She hurried home in time to hear the phone ring. It was my cross-country coach asking if I had returned from practice. "George, I know my daughter," she told him. My mom knew that something was terribly wrong and demanded that he call the police immediately.

A massive search was mobilized, without such technological advances as AMBER Alert. The local police officers awoke to realize that one of their own was missing, and that they had little to go on to mobilize a search. But they made so much happen that day. They didn't wait 24 hours. They didn't hesitate. They got right to work, using every source available. Everyone came to my little hometown to search for me.

A law enforcement helicopter spotted me as my abductor held me hostage in the woods. Law enforcement officers invaded the area and rescued me. But those 4 to 5 hours I was held captive had been terrifying—I was raped, strangled, buried under some brush, and shot.

At the hospital I received amazing care by people with big hearts. Even though the actual medical procedures usually hurt and seemed to last forever, the doctors and nurses always put my well-being first. I am so grateful to them for the care they gave me those 13 days.

Leaving the hospital proved to be a bump in the road I wasn't expecting—the day I left the hospital was actually very difficult. I was so happy to be going home. I felt such triumph in how far I'd come. Yet, I was terribly sad to leave those I had come to depend on. And believe it or not, I was nervous about returning to the life I led a few weeks earlier. I was filled with so many emotions: Excitement. Joy. Anxiety. Peace. Anticipation. Fear. You may have had similar emotions when you returned home, or even different ones. I found out later that this is normal.

I did not realize this at first, but families suffer the experience with you—it's kind of a ripple effect. It happened to you—and it happened to them. Even in a tightly bonded family, you may feel estranged from everyone around you. This too is normal. I found it helpful to find my own space and to set boundaries, to figure out what I needed and tell others what it was. If you need family constantly around you, so be it. If not, that's okay, too. Just remember they love you, they looked for you, prayed for you, and did everything under the sun to find you.

But just as we are different individuals, how we cope and deal with adversities is different—and sometimes different than even we expected. Some family members may want to talk about what's happened, and others may not. You may want to talk, or you may not. Everyone deals with their experience in their own way. The important thing is to communicate what you want and what you need.

> **❝** I have two older brothers who have handled this experience in totally different ways. A while after I came home, I went to them and said, 'Look, we've never talked about what happened, but I want you to know that I am here. Ask me anything you want, whenever you want.' One took me up on that and asked me a lot of questions. My other brother and I have never talked about it to this day. Both ways are fine. I'm still their sister, which will never change. **❞**

Remember that you are not responsible for anyone's recovery but your own. I learned this early on as well. You may worry about your family and others, but ultimately you cannot control how they deal with things. Be sure your needs are met first so you can function, heal, and thrive.

Along the road to recovery, I found that there were a lot of potential detours that I had to avoid. I had to face my abductor at the trial, which I had never anticipated. I had to appear before the Parole Board, which was something I never really thought about, either. To this day, certain things bring back memories of my abduction—men with red hair, the smell of grass. You, too, may experience things that trigger memories of what happened. And it seems like they surface when you least expect them.

> **" How have I gotten to where I am today? How have I gotten through adversities? My faith. My desire. My determination. I figured if what I endured was supposed to kill me, I would have died the day it happened. But I'm here. Life goes on. And I choose to go with it."**

No one can tell you the best way to recover from what's happened. No one has the perfect answer about how to get through the incredibly imperfect mess that you've gone through. For me, the process was to physically heal first. Then came the emotional healing. The key is your desire—your choice—to want to heal. To be better. To live. Only then can you move on.

All of us who helped to put together this book can only give you suggestions about what worked for each of us—what made sense for each of us—based upon what we experienced. The reality is that it is up to you. You have the choice to move on. You have the choice to deal with this in a way that is beneficial for you. You have the opportunity to take something awful and figure out how it affects your life, not directs it.

FINDING YOUR STRENGTH

It is not easy. Some days are more of a struggle than others. And though sometimes it feels like it will never get better, eventually, if you keep working on it, it will get better. Although at times you may feel that what's happened to you has set you so far behind, it actually may have pushed you far ahead. You've been given tremendous exposure to a different view of life that so many never see. You have gained so much strength and wisdom and may not realize it. Instead of looking back on what you lost, look at what you've gained. Find your strength.

Magic

" If you think you aren't strong or worth anything, think about the fact that you get out of bed everyday, right? You live everyday, right? You're contributing to life, right? That's power. That's progress. That's strength. That's empowerment. Undoubtedly what happened to you has had a huge impact on you and your family, but it represents a mere fraction of what you are capable of accomplishing, of who you are, and most of all, what you can overcome.

Whatever happens from here on out, know that most everything can be okay. You are amazing. No matter what happens, you've won. Don't forget that. Ever. "

Space for your thoughts:

SECTION 5: THE NEW NORMAL

What you have experienced will, in some respects, change you for the rest of your life. Things cannot go back to exactly the way they were before your abduction. You may feel like you were forced to become an adult long before you should have. You may feel like your home life has been altered in some respect, whether it be a big change or a minor one. You may feel you have learned life lessons that not many others have learned. You may have a different outlook on things—a different appreciation for small things in life—a new perspective and resolve.

None of these feelings are out of the ordinary. They are part of finding the "new normal."

> **"** It took a long time to get to a 'new normal' with my mother. It was not as if there was a 'normal' that had just had a small glitch and then was to resume. I had my 'normal,' my mom had hers, and we had to somehow create a new reality that was about the present and future and not only about the lost shared past. **"** — Sarah

SETTING BOUNDARIES

It's not easy for anyone to adjust when an abducted young person returns home. Everyone has new thoughts and new fears that were not part of everyday life before. Some families become very overprotective of their children. Some family members try to gain their own "15 minutes of fame" out of a child's experience. Some families bond tightly together in the face of this kind of crisis. Others find that it threatens to tear them apart.

Your whole family will go on a journey towards empowerment. In some sense, the experience happened to all of you. But it's very important to remember that you can only be responsible for your own recovery. You did not cause this event to happen, and you cannot fix the damage that resulted from it. The best you can do is help your family figure out what you need from them and set the boundaries.

Talk with them about your needs and desires. Talk with them about what you need to help get you through this. Be honest with your thoughts. Some of us found that our brothers, sisters, or other relatives were good resources for us, and that they could act as mediators to help protect us from people who did not have our best interests in mind. They listened to us when we needed an ear, and helped us think though problems and how to face them.

" What did bother me was when people would find out that it was my father who abducted me, and they would assume that it was not a bad thing. I know that I was one of the lucky ones because even though my dad was wrong to take me, when I was with him I was at least physically safe. But it still took a chunk of my life away, and it hurt me in many ways. I've had a lot to deal with because of it. People need to understand that no matter who took you or what happened while you were gone, it's still a traumatic event. No one's story is any less valid than anyone else's. " — Sam

We know that each of our family issues and dynamics were different than yours will be when you are making your way through your journey. And although we have said it many times, the most important thing is to ask for help when you need it, verbalize what you need, and set boundaries and expectations so everyone knows what is best for each other.

Just as you may need to ask your family for help or to give you space to figure things out, allow them to do the same. Take your time.

RETURNING TO SCHOOL

Returning to school can be a major milestone in your recovery. There are a number of decisions you will have to make based on the circumstances of your abduction and what you and people you trust have decided is best for your situation.

Don't feel like you need to make all of these decisions on your own. In fact, make sure that you talk with your parents and maybe other adults you trust about what makes sense for you.

> "In the beginning I didn't discuss things with my family. We didn't talk about what had happened. I just wanted to be normal with them. I thought, 'I'm still me, just treat me as I am.' For me it was about needing to feel like I had control over talking about a time when all control was taken away from me. My family let me set the pace, and that was good."
> — Tamara

Some of us returned to school right away because we needed the interaction and the normalcy. Others needed more time in a less visible environment to let the healing process begin. Whatever you decide, make sure it is a plan you and the people you trust are comfortable with.

Here are some options you might want to consider:

>> Go back to the same school right away.

>> Change schools.

>> Wait out the remainder of one school year and start the next.

>> Homeschool.

>> Go back half days at first to ease into the transition.

If you and your parents decide that it is best for you to return to school, talk with teachers and counselors to help decide what is best for you and how to go about it.

This is true for a school that you had been attending before your abduction, as well as a new school that you might attend. Meeting with the teachers before you return to school will give you an opportunity to help them understand what you need and what to expect when you are back in the classroom. It may also be an opportunity for you to ask the teachers and counselors what other kids in school are talking about and prepare yourself for the potential questions from them. It may be a good way to help you feel comfortable and ease back into the classroom.

When you do go back to school, there will be elements you can't control. People may look at you as you walk down the halls. You may hear whispers behind your back. Other students, and even some teachers, may ask you what seem like ridiculous questions. These can just be normal reactions from people. They may be happy to see that you are home safe and that you are okay. They may be worried about what to say to you right now. Try not to read too deeply into anything. Surround yourself with people who truly care about you at school to help you make the transition back to this part of your life.

If you and your parents decide that it is best for you to be homeschooled or postpone your return to school, make sure that you find some positive, constructive outlets so you are not isolated from friends. See about returning to a music or dance class that you participated in before. Get involved in sports activities, school clubs, or something else positive for yourself that can help you begin to move towards a new normal in life.

> **The best advice the counselors gave the other students was to take their cues from me. If I talked about it, it was okay to talk about it. If I didn't, then they shouldn't bring it up.**
> — Maggie

CELEBRITY STATUS

Be prepared to live in a fishbowl when you get home. For at least a while, it's going to feel like everyone is watching you, scrutinizing your decisions, and broadcasting everything from your bad hair days to your prom date. Sometimes it's a result of all the media attention. Sometimes it's just because everyone in a small town knows you now and was part of the effort to bring you home. Sometimes you may like the attention, but most of the time it becomes a nuisance and feels like an invasion of privacy.

> "In other people's minds, I'll always be 14 years old like the day I came home. But you have an opportunity to show them that's not who you are. You have so much more to offer. If you give them a chance to get to know you, you can change that image." — Elizabeth

This is not an easy thing to manage, but try to get used to it. Talk with your parents or a trusted adult if the attention becomes too much for you. Ask for their guidance and advice on how to respond, what to say, and how to act. In time you will learn how to handle people who are polite about honoring your privacy and those who are not. For us, this was an opportunity to change our image from being a "victim" to a person who has overcome major challenges in life and gone on to do much more. Believe it or not, a time will come in your life when there are people around you who know nothing about the abduction. You will be known as a whole person apart from these circumstances.

> "I learned some things in the process. Do not get discouraged with your situation. Time does heal. You may never understand why other people don't understand what you have been through, so don't worry about it." — Lindsey

Space for your thoughts:

ALICIA'S STORY

Welcome home! You are one tough kid—you've survived. You're probably a big ball of emotions right now. You may feel sad, angry, relieved, afraid, or guilty. You might even have all of these emotions at the same time—that is perfectly normal. There is no definite way you should feel. But one thing you certainly shouldn't feel is guilt. You did nothing wrong. Over and over again you will hear people say, This isn't your fault," and "You're the innocent victim." Though this may be hard to grasp, it's true!

What gives me the credibility to say this? Like you, I am a survivor. And honestly, I just forgave myself this past year. I finally said to my mother, "I really am not to blame!" It took a very long time, 5 years to be exact, but it finally sank in and a huge weight was lifted from me. I finally felt free. Wow, what a glorious feeling!

My name is Alicia. I am a college sophomore studying forensic psychology and am 19 years old. I want to tell you about my experience because I think it is important that you realize there are people out there who prey on children, and that there are things that you can do to protect yourself—rights that you have— to help you move forward in your journey from abduction to empowerment.

When I was 13 years old I was lured away from the safety of my home by an Internet predator. Of course my parents warned me about strangers online. But to me this guy wasn't a stranger. I thought he was my one true friend. He made me feel loved, beautiful, special, and unique which, when it comes down to it, is how we all want to feel. This is why I imagine that I felt obligated to meet him.

He took me to his home a few States away and kept me chained for 4 days. I had a locking dog collar around my neck with a chain that was bolted to the floor beside his bed. He abused me. I had nothing to eat my entire captivity. I was terrified. I wasn't sure what was going to happen. He threatened me constantly and at times carried through on his threats.

The day I was rescued, he was at work. I heard loud noises, the door crashing down, and then people screaming, "We have guns!" I was so frightened. At that moment, I was not sure what was happening, whether my abductor had sent someone to hurt me or if law enforcement had found me. I was terrified at the sight of the guns pointed towards me. I was so afraid until I saw the big bold yellow letters FBI on the back of their jackets. At that point I knew that I had been saved.

That first night I was placed in a foster home until my parents could arrive. I felt that I was being swept away by all the emotions and activity, and it was all I could do to hold on. I was also really anxious to see my parents. Because of all the media coverage, it was decided that it was safest for my parents to fly up to see me the next morning. In the confusion, no one told me they weren't coming that night. As I waited for them, I began to wonder whether they even wanted me home at all. When I finally did see them the next morning, my dad gave me the most amazing hug in the world. You could just about hear the Hallelujah chorus. It was such a happy reunion and was the first time I felt safe in 5 days.

ARRIVING HOME

I was like a big ball of emotions when I first came home. A lot of times my feelings were misplaced. I was angry about what had happened. Sometimes I would release my emotions on whoever was closest to me at that moment, even though it might not have had anything to do with them. I wasn't sure how I should feel. It's very hard to get a check on your emotions because they seem to be all over the place.

A big problem for me was that I thought I was going to be just fine as soon as I got home again. I didn't know I was going to keep hurting. I wasn't all that familiar with post-traumatic stress disorder—not until this happened. The most common things became triggers, reminding me of what I had just been through—tollbooths and Coca-Cola cans for example. I am still learning what triggers me today.

" The reality is that even though you're a child, you've just been through a very adult situation, and that is extremely difficult. "

IT'S NOT YOUR FAULT

It took me a while to realize that what happened to me was not my fault. This is a hard thing to realize. The reality is that there are people who prey on children—especially on the Internet—and that they know how to lure children away from the safety of their homes. They know what to say to children to make them feel special. They know how to get children to reveal more about themselves than they should. They know how to befriend and "groom" children to make them feel safe. A lot of kids feel like it is their fault and that their parents are going to be mad at them. But remember that your parents searched for you—they worried about you when you were gone and wanted to bring you home—and they can help you down the road to recovery.

It was difficult when I finally got back home. I had changed and my life had changed. I started to rely a lot on humor to help me cope, but it was a very dark humor. I lost a lot of my shyness. I learned that it is important to talk to someone you trust about your feelings, and I am continuing to learn to ask for help if needed.

Many of us turn to our parents in times of need, but sometimes some of us need to talk with other people who can help us work through our emotions. Seeking professional help to deal with all of the emotions and feelings is important, even though many of us may be uncomfortable thinking that we need to see someone like a "shrink." Don't turn your back on this option. I didn't and it helped me.

"I even asked the police whether they could write me an excuse for missing school. It seems kind of silly now, but you can get so confused about what is happening around you."

Another thing that was difficult was figuring out what to do about school. I worried about school the whole time I was gone. School was all I could think about. As it turned out, my parents made the decision to home-school me to protect me and keep me safe. They thought it was best that I finish out eighth grade at home with my mom, and then start fresh the next year.

When I went back to school for the ninth grade, I thought it would be a chance for a fresh start because it was a new school. But instead of getting "Hey, aren't you the new girl?" people asked inappropriate questions and made inappropriate comments. Not only that, but because people felt they knew what had happened to me and knew about the darkest corners of my life, they thought they could share their traumatic experiences with me. At first I felt obligated to listen and to try to help them. But that became a huge responsibility—trying to deal with my problems while hearing about theirs.

FINDING A BALANCE

Although it was hard emotionally I had to overcome the negative comments and images that others incorrectly placed on me. I threw myself into dozens of clubs and activities, partly to stay busy so I didn't have to think about things, and partly because I wanted to give people a chance to know me for something positive. I didn't want to be "that girl" anymore.

That was good in a sense, but it also took its toll. I would come home at night exhausted and just think, "What am I doing to myself?"

REBUILDING TRUST

So much trust is broken when you've gone through this kind of situation— trust in other people, trust in yourself and your ability to make decisions, trust in the world. I remember when I was little, I actually thought the world was like a Disney movie, where people were so happy that they would just burst into song. My abduction made me realize that there is evil in the world—and sometimes you can't hide from it. You have to learn to live in a world where that kind of evil exists, and find a way to do something to make it a better place.

> "If I were to give some advice, I would say that the key is to find a healthy balance. It may be difficult to do this on your own, so make sure you ask others you trust to help."

First, you have to start rebuilding trust in yourself, then you can begin to trust others again. My family had trust issues with me, as well. My parents had the most difficult time giving me privacy because they were so concerned about me. My mom slept with the Internet cord underneath her pillow for a year. That couldn't have been comfortable! Even now, anytime I am on the computer, they want to know whom I am talking to and they always seem to magically be in the same room.

Before I was kidnapped, I had been really shy and quiet, and most of the friends I had were people that I met online. After, my parents were scared to death (for good reason!) of letting me on the computer, so I lost those friendships. Their overprotectiveness was legitimate, given everything we went through. It just didn't make it any easier to understand. It's been a long, slow process of working out how I can have freedom and be a normal teenager, but still be safe.

> **"You might go back and forth between the negative and the positive actions and emotions, and that's understandable— don't beat yourself up about it. But look for the good things. The other things can numb the pain for a while, but they don't fix it. You end up worse off than where you started."**

MAKING GOOD CHOICES

When something like this happens, there is a void left in your life. You basically have two choices: You can fill it with negative things, like alcohol, drugs, or promiscuity; or you can fill it with good works and a good heart. It's not easy to make the right choices. You're still a kid, even though this very adult thing has happened to you.

I made the decision to take this negative experience and turn it into a positive one. I made the decision that I am not going to let it define who I am and dictate the rest of my life. And I have made the decision that this experience will empower me to speak out in order to protect other children. I have become a strong advocate for children, particularly as related to Internet safety. Almost every Friday, I go into schools and talk to kids about my experiences.

Though exhausting, I also find it extremely cathartic. Talking about what happened to me and saving kids from going through my horrors—Wow, what a miracle! I realized at some point that I would go through the whole experience again, if I would end up in the same place, because of the good that has come out of it. I've talked to kids who changed their behavior because of my story. If I can save just one life, ONE, then it's all been worth it. On the days when it is a struggle to get up and keep going, I think about the fact that I did survive, and there has to be a reason for that. There's something more for me to do in this world and I want to do it!

My commitment has allowed me to educate the public about ways to protect children and inform elected officials about the dangers lurking out there for children. When I think about it, it is amazing that here I am, 19-year-old Alicia, and I have something important to say that can help others. People are listening and changing things in society so that kids are kept safe. This has been an incredible journey for me.

Alicia

> "Not all of us choose to go down the path that I have chosen. I chose this for me because it is what I need, it is my passion, and it is my way of taking control and empowering myself to move forward in my journey. It is also about building trust again—in yourself and with others. And although the journey can be very hard, in the end you can find a path that is good for you—you can make the choice—for you are a survivor and you will come through this!"

A LETTER TO PARENTS

Dear Parents,

As sons and daughters who were abducted, thank you for everything you did to bring us back safely. We know that the experience was extremely hard on you and on your entire family. It is something we all wish had not happened, but it did. Your family will not be as it once was; it is going to be different now. We will all struggle to find the new normal in our lives. But we know that our return would not have happened if you had not been looking for us, and for that we are grateful—even if we can't always say it.

Together we can and will get through this. We will begin to reconnect in a way that is positive for all of us. It will not be easy. It is a long road ahead. We ask that you continue to help us through the process and be patient with us.

There may be bumps along the way. It is not our fault that this happened, nor is it yours. Things may be different than before, but different is not always a bad thing. This experience can make us all stronger. It can make us appreciate each other more. And it can help us to move in directions that we never thought possible.

We ask that you help us build trust again—in ourselves, and in others. Please make sure that we have someone to help us through our journey from abduction to empowerment—someone who we trust—someone who can help us deal with all that has happened in a constructive manner. Help us find someone who is just for us—someone we know we can trust to whom we can say anything and everything we need to say.

There are some things we don't want you to know. Please don't take this personally. It's not that we don't trust you. It's because we want to protect you. Let us do that. And at the same time, please find someone to help you take care of yourselves, and of our brothers and sisters. This happened to all of us.

We hope that you will find our words and stories comforting as they tell you that moving forward is possible, even if we move in another direction than before our abduction. Once again we thank you, for your patience, support, and help in our journey.

Maria   Sam   Elizabeth

Alicia   Juman

> " I realized at some point that I would go through the whole experience again, if I had to, because good has come out of it. I've talked to kids who have changed their behavior because of my story. If just one of those kids was saved from an Internet abduction, then it's all been worth it. On the days when it's a struggle to get up and keep going, I think about the fact that I did survive, and there has to be a reason for that. There's something more for me to do. I want to do it. " — Alicia

WHERE TO FIND MORE HELP

Everyone who has been abducted and returned has their own experiences and their own needs. There are probably many times that you wish you had somewhere to turn for support as you move down the road to finding the new normal for yourself. Individuals whom you may have turned to in the past might not be the ones you feel comfortable talking with right now. You may need answers to specific questions, information about resources that might be available, suggestions on where else you can turn.

The most important thing is to find someone who you trust to talk with:

>> Your parents.

>> A professional counselor or therapist.

>> Someone facing similar circumstances.

>> A trusted adult like a relative, lifelong babysitter, or family friend.

>> A member of clergy.

>> A school counselor, teacher, scout leader, or coach—someone whom you know and trust.

Other resources are available to offer information and support for families of missing children. Here are some places you can turn to for more help:

- **The Office of Juvenile Justice and Delinquency Prevention** has been committed to youth for more than 30 years. One of the most important goals of OJJDP is to keep children safe through such programs as the Internet Crimes Against Children Program and the AMBER Alert Program. To access information about the resources of OJJDP, visit their Web site at **http://www.ojp.usdoj.gov/ojjdp.**

- **The National Center for Missing & Exploited Children** (NCMEC) was established in 1984 to help prevent child abduction and sexual exploitation; find missing children; and assist victims of child abduction and sexual exploitation, their families, and the professionals who serve them. To access their resources, visit their Web site at **www.missingkids.com** or call NCMEC at 800–THE–LOST (800–843–5678).

- Every State, plus the District of Columbia, Puerto Rico, and Canada, has a **Missing Children Clearinghouse**, which is designed to provide support and assistance to families of missing children. You can find a listing of every State Clearinghouse on the NCMEC Web site at **www.missingkids.com**. On the left side of the page, click on the tab for resources for parents and guardians.

- **The Association of Missing and Exploited Children's Organizations** is a membership organization of nonprofit local agencies in the United States and Canada that provide services to the families of missing children. They can help with resource referrals as well as advocacy, poster and flyer development and dissemination, and aid to local law enforcement. Visit their Web site at **www.amecoinc.org** or call them at 877–263–2620.

- **Team H.O.P.E.** (Help Offering Parents Empowerment) is a parent mentoring and support program for families of missing children. Made up of parent volunteers, Team H.O.P.E. provides mentoring services, counseling, and emotional support for both parents and other family members. Volunteers can be reached at 866–305–HOPE (4673).

- **Take Root** provides support and assistance to children who have been abducted by a family member. Take Root can be reached at 800–ROOT–ORG or by visiting their Web site at **www.takeroot.org.**

- Through the **Office for Victims of Crime**, all States, the District of Columbia, the Commonwealth of Puerto Rico, the U.S. Virgin Islands, and the territories of American Samoa, Guam, and the Commonwealth of the Northern Mariana Islands receive victim assistance grants to support direct services to crime victims. Grants support domestic violence shelters; rape crisis centers; child abuse programs; and victim service units in law enforcement agencies, prosecutors' offices, hospitals, and social service agencies. These programs provide crisis intervention, counseling, emergency shelter, criminal justice advocacy, emergency transportation, and related services. Through Victims of Crime Act funding, State agencies within the United States and U.S. territories have established compensation programs to reimburse crime victims and assistance programs to offer victim services. Information about these services can be found at **http://www.ojp.usdoj.gov/ovc/help/links.htm.**

NOTES

This document is one of three important publications developed by the Department of Justice to assist and support children and families who have suffered the trauma of a child abduction. In 1997 the Department of Justice worked with parents of abducted children to create a guide to help families cope with the loss of a child, titled *When Your Child Is Missing: A Family Survival Guide.* In 2007, the Department of Justice worked with the left-behind brothers and sisters of abducted children to make sure they are no longer the forgotten victims. With their assistance, a guide titled *What About Me: Coping With the Abduction of a Brother or Sister* was written and a video produced to help brothers and sisters cope. All three publications are important tools not only for families, but for friends, acquaintances, and professionals who deal with the abduction of a child. All three publications are available from the National Criminal Justice Reference Service at **www.ncjrs.org.**

ACKNOWLEDGMENTS

A project like this takes many hands to turn it from a vision to reality. No one person could have done this on his or her own.

We would like to thank personally several individuals for their contributions to this document. Our thanks first go to J. Robert Flores, the Administrator of the Office of Juvenile Justice and Delinquency Prevention, for his leadership and commitment to children and families. Many thanks go to Ron Laney, Associate Administrator of the Child Protection Division, Office of Juvenile Justice and Delinquency Prevention, U.S. Department of Justice, not only for his leadership on this project but for his tireless commitment to helping children. We want to thank Helen Connelly of Fox Valley Technical College for her direction, guidance, and compassion. Thank you to Cheri Hoffman, Julie Kenniston, and Lori St. Onge for walking with us throughout the process. Finally, thanks to Katherine Lenard of FasterKitty, LLC for envisioning and designing the final product. You all played such an important role in making this document a reality! We cannot thank you enough.

Many other people were part of this process as well and deserve our gratitude: Harriet Heiberg and Tom Weeden of Fox Valley Technical College; Catherine Doyle of OJJDP; Tom Cullen of Lockheed Martin; Lynn Miller; Liss Hart-Haviv from Take Root; Nancy Sabin of the Jacob Wetterling Foundation; and Abby Potash from Team HOPE. Thank you for working with us to communicate this important message and these words of hope and encouragement.

YOUR STORY

www.ingramcontent.com/pod-product-compliance
Lightning Source LLC
Chambersburg PA
CBHW071623170526
45166CB00003B/1171